D1378797

Odd or Even in a Monstrous Season

by Spencer Brinker

Consultant:
Kimberly Brenneman, PhD
National Institute for Early Education Research
Rutgers University
New Brunswick, New Jersey

New York, New York

Credits

Publisher: Kenn Goin
Editorial Director: Adam Siegel
Senior Editor: Joyce Tavolacci
Creative Director: Spencer Brinker
Photo Illustrations: Kim Jones

Library of Congress Cataloging-in-Publication Data

Brinker, Spencer, author.
  Odd or even in a monstrous season / by Spencer Brinker ; consultant: Kimberly
Brenneman, PhD, National Institute for Early Education Research, Rutgers University, New
Brunswick, New Jersey.
      pages cm. — (Spooky math)
  Audience: Ages 4–8.
  Includes bibliographical references.
  ISBN-13: 978-1-62724-331-5 (library binding)
  ISBN-10: 1-62724-331-3 (library binding)
  1. Cardinal numbers—Juvenile literature. 2. Numbers, Natural—Juvenile literature. 3.
Monsters—Juvenile literature. I. Title.
  QA248.B85 2015
  513—dc23
                                       2014012033

For more information, write to Bearport Publishing Company, Inc., 45 West 21st Street,
Suite 3B, New York, New York 10010. Printed in the United States of America.

10 9 8 7 6 5 4 3 2 1

Contents

A Monstrous Season

Meet Elsie the Even.
She's a monster, it's true.

4

Here's Onslow the Odd.
He's a monster who's blue.

5

A monster who's even?
An odd monster—how?

6

What on earth does that mean?
Let's take a look now.

Even numbers end with
0, 2, 4, 6, or 8.

Elsie smiles and says,
"These numbers are great!"

10 12 24 36 58

9

Odd numbers end with
1, 3, 5, 7, or 9.

Onslow loves these a lot.
He says, "They're super fine."

Dividing a number by two tells a lot.

If a number is odd,
there's something left over.

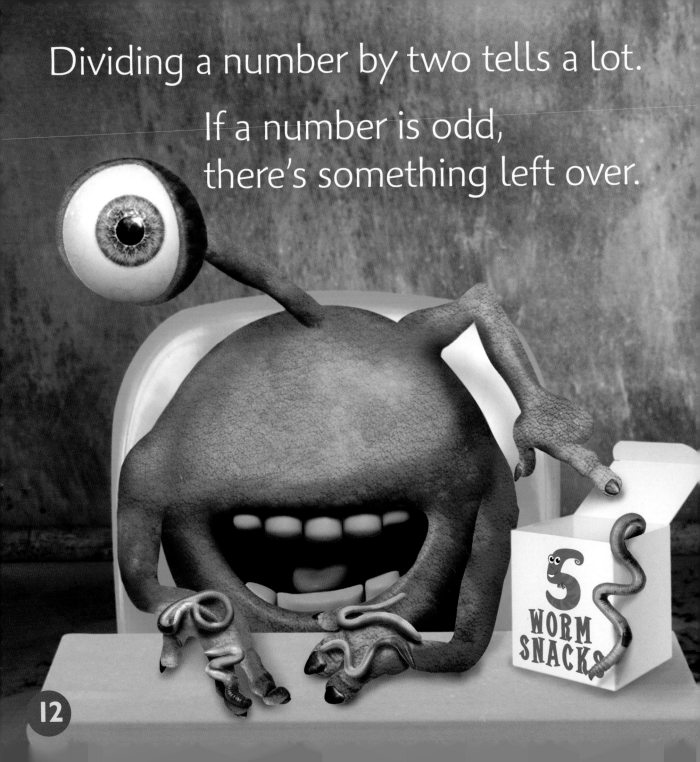

If a number is even,
there definitely is not.

WORM
SNACKS

13

Look at this notebook.
See the numbers in blue.

Which are even? Which are odd?
Check the end for a clue.

even!

28   46

55   odd!

99

ANSWER: 2, 10, 28, and 46 are even. 5, 13, 55, and 99 are odd.

Elsie is even.
That's all that she likes.

If she counted the wheels, she'd pick which monster bikes?

It's only the odd groups
that Onslow would choose.

Which ones would he pick
when he's shopping for shoes?

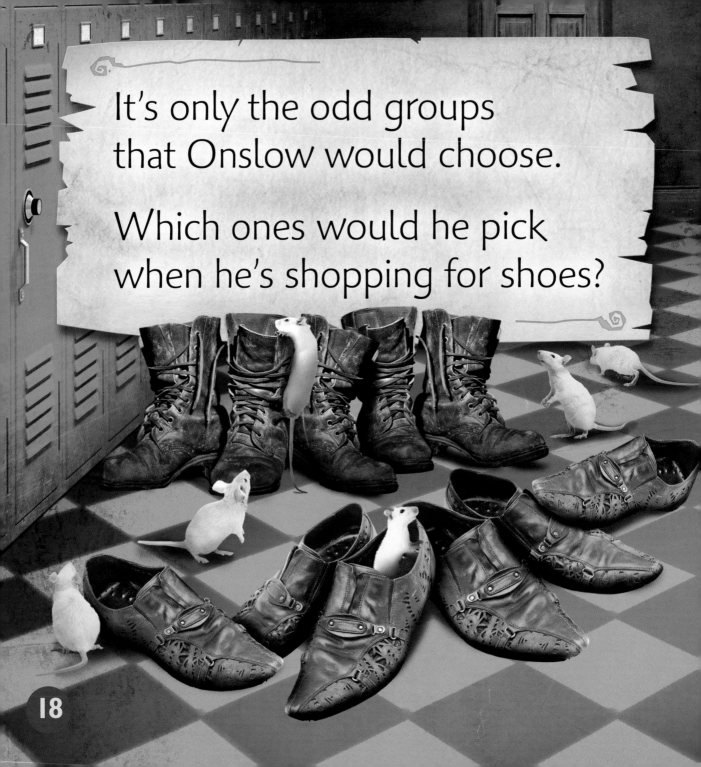

ANSWER: Onslow would choose the red and purple groups of shoes because they have odd numbers of shoes: 5 and 7.

Elsie eats flowers
(and sometimes a bee).

Which ones would she choose?
Count the petals to see.

Onslow loves baked goods—
a real monster treat.

Count the beetles to see
which cookies he'd eat.

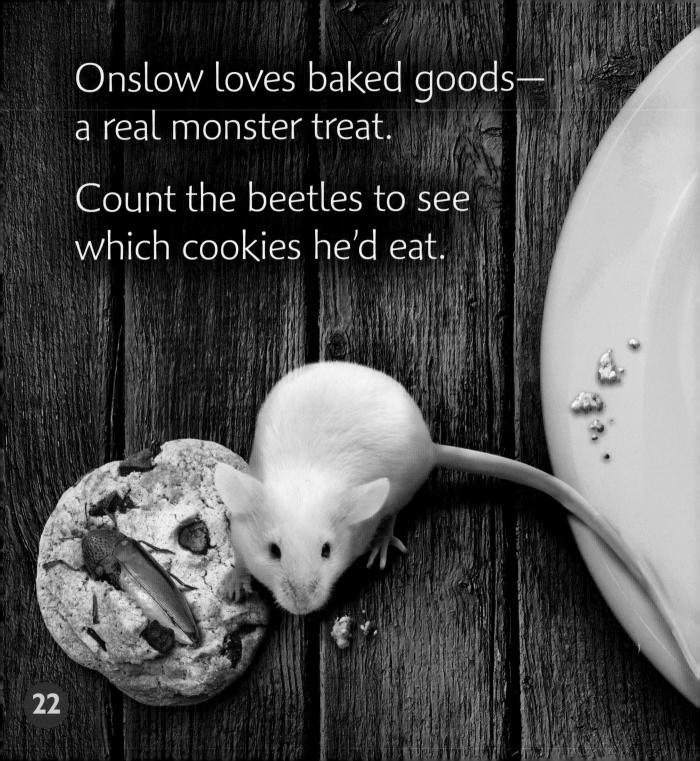

ANSWER: Onslow would eat the cookies with the green, purple, and red beetles because they are odd numbers: 1, 3, and 5.

This friend isn't cuddly.
He's slimy and wet.

Count all his long arms.
He's which monster's pet?

ANSWER: The octopus is Elsie's pet because
it has 8 arms and 8 is an even number.

This bird is quite creepy,
and so is its song.

Is it Onslow's or Elsie's?
To whom does it belong?

ANSWER: The bird belongs to Onslow since it has 3 wings,
5 legs, and 9 claws, and those are all odd numbers.

27

Elsie and Onslow
go to a school called "Boo!"

BOO ELEMENTARY SCHOOL

Name: Elsie the Even

Classroom: 2424

Birthday: 02-14-2004

6 8 4 2 6 0 4 8 6 2

Can you find the odd numbers
and the even ones, too?

BOO ELEMENTARY SCHOOL

Name: Onslow the Odd

Classroom: 1919

Birthday: 11-13-2003

9 5 9 7 9 1 0 9 3 9 5

ANSWER: All of the numbers on Elsie's ID card are even except for 1.
All of the numbers on Onslow's ID card are odd except for 2 and 0.

Goodbye even Elsie.
Farewell odd Onslow.

These monsters sort numbers
wherever they go.

Read More

Harris, Trudy. *Splitting the Herd: A Corral of Odds and Evens.* Minneapolis, MN: Millbrook (2008).

Mattern, Joanne. *Even or Odd? (Little World Math Concepts).* Vero Beach, FL: Rourke (2011).

Learn More Online

To learn more about odd and even numbers, visit **www.bearportpublishing.com/SpookyMath**

About the Author

Spencer Brinker lives and works in New York City. Since it's a big and busy city, sometimes life is odd, but Spencer does his best to stay calm and even.